This delightful and fun story is for every young child. It will teach them all a lesson on acceptance.

It will show them that we can learn no matter what the color of our skin is or what we look like.

Once upon a time, there were three beautiful learning butterflies flying in the garden.

One was **Pink**,
One was **Yellow**,
And One was **Purple**.

The Pink Butterfly said,

"I have an idea."

The Yellow Butterfly asked,

"What's the idea?"

The Pink Butterfly said,

"Let's fly to all of the beautiful colored flowers and see if they will help us Count to 20.

We need to Count to 20 to go to first grade.

The Purple Butterfly said,

"That is a great idea."

The butterflies stopped at the Pink Flower and asked, "Will you help us Count to 20?"

The Pink Flower said,
"I will only help the Pink Butterfly,
sorry."

The butterflies flew off sad.

The Yellow Butterfly said, "Don't be sad; let's ask the Yellow Flower."

The butterflies went to the Yellow Flower and asked, "Will you help us Count to 20? So, we can go to first grade."

The Yellow Flower answered, "I will only help the Yellow Butterfly."
And so, the butterflies flew away sad again.

"Who will help us?" asked the Pink Butterfly. The Purple Butterfly replied, "Don't be sad; we can ask the Purple Flower."

The butterflies flew over to the Purple Flower and asked, "Will you help us count to 20? Because we need to go to first grade."

The Purple Flower answered, "No, I will only help the Purple Butterfly." And so, the butterflies flew away, sad again.

"I will help you."

"Who are you?"

They looked up
and saw this beautiful
Pink, Yellow, and Purple
flower.

So, the butterflies flew over to

the Colorful Flower

and it said,

"It doesn't matter

what color you are,

we all can learn to count."

They all learned to count to 20

And then happily flew away

to first grade.

The End

I dedicate this book first and foremost to God.

I also would like to acknowledge my awesome team at Jazzy Kitty Publications. Mr. LeRoy for his vision and page design/illustrations. Anelda for her kindness and patience.

I would like to thank Lee Horton, aka Peanut, for taking my photographs and motivating me to be the best author.

And Last but not least, my wonderful parents Jamie and Allen Fair, for believing in me.

ABOUT THE AUTHOR

Anesha Joann Davis was born on September 5, 1989, in Wilmington, Delaware, but was raised in Gastonia, North Carolina. She was first introduced to writing at the age of 14 through song lyrics. This is **Anesha's** second book. Her first book is Baby Tiny Steps.

The Learning Butterflies

By Anesha Davis

Published by Jazzy Kitty Publications

New Castle, DE 19720

Tel: 877.782.5550

Website: http://www.jazzykittypublications.com

Copyright © 2021 Anesha Davis

ISBN: 978-1-954425-30-9

Library of Congress Control Number: 2021910413

Additional Credits: Book Cover created by Anelda Attaway of Jazzy Kitty Publications; Cover illustrated by LeRoy Grayson (Headshot Photo/About the Author) by Lee Horton. Logo Designs – Inside the book by Bryant Vickers and back cover by Andre M. Saunders.

All rights are explicitly reserved worldwide. This book is protected under the copyright laws of the United States of America. This book may not be copied or reprinted for commercial profit or net income. The purpose of short quotations or occasional page copying for personal or group study is permitted and promoted. Permission to copy will be freely granted upon request for Worldwide Distribution. Printed and published in the United States of America. Created Jazzy Kitty Greetings Marketing & Publishing, LLC dba Jazzy Kitty Publications are utilizing Microsoft Publishing and BookCoverly Software.

www.ingramcontent.com/pod-product-compliance
Lightning Source LLC
Chambersburg PA
CBHW040020300426
43673CB00106B/306